Words Against the Void:
Poems by an Existential Psychologist
(Revised & Expanded Edition)

by
Tom Greening

University
PROFESSORS PRESS

Colorado Springs, CO
www.universityprofessorspress.com

Words Against the Void: Poems by an Existential Psychologist
By Tom Greening

Revised and Expanded Edition First Published

ISBN-13: 978-1-939686-20-6

University Professors Press
Colorado Springs, CO

Cover Design by Laura Ross, 2008
Cover Photo by Yurok from Shutterstock.com

The original version of *Words Against the Void: Poems by an Existential Psychologist* was published by University of the Rockies Press. The revised and expanded edition is published with permission from University Professors Press.

The poems "Freedom vs. Determinism," "Intuition," and "Psychology" were originally published in *Dialogues: Therapeutic Applications of Existential Philosophy*. Reprinted with permission.

The poems "For Ronnie Lang," "Awareness," "Cure," "Brain Chemistry," "Matter," and "Research" were previously published in the *Journal of Humanistic Psychology*. Reprinted with permission.

The poem "Managed Care" was originally published in the *Independent Practitioner*, the newsletter of Division 42 of the American Psychological Association (Psychologists in Independent Practice).

Tom Greening is a witty, courageous, and insidiously brilliant critic of psychiatric fraud and folly – and our pathologized society. This short book is full of truth and wisdom and is a deceptively easy read. Laugh and learn.

Thomas Szasz, MD
Author, *The Myth of Mental Illness*

Poetry has the capacity of expressing thoughts, feelings, and experiences in a manner both unique and profound. The distinguished psychotherapist Dr. Tom Greening has written a bevy of brilliant poems that reveal grief and joy, anguish and humor, and depths of meaning and insight that would be inconceivable through any other medium.

Stanley Krippner, PhD
Co-Author, *Haunted by Combat:*
Understanding PTSD in War Veterans

I suppose you could, on a cold winter night, curl up in front of a fireplace and read these poems by Tom Greening. However, this could be dangerous to your psyche because the incongruence between place and poems would be too great. These poems, despite their self-deprecating humor, laser right through our defenses and reveal us to ourselves. If we are flying too high, these poems bring us down to earth. If we are feeling too low, they raise us up. If we think we are intellectuals who have it all figured out, they make a face at us. If we are panicked by our ignorance, they walk by our side and tell us jokes to cheer us up. Tom Greening and Herbert Lochenkopf pretend to be fools, clowns, jesters; but if you get their message, you will stop laughing. Laughter and tears just don't mix.

David N. Elkins, PhD, Professor Emeritus of Psychology, Pepperdine University

Tom Greening's poems are a joy – and that ain't no ploy! A pioneer in the "Humoristic" side of Humanistic Psychology, Tom has for decades now, restored wit, wisdom, and absurdity to a high art.

Kirk Schneider, PhD
Editor, Journal of Humanistic Psychology
Author of *Existential-Integrative Psychotherapy*
and *Rediscovery of Awe*

In these poems, Tom unwraps his wounded self in order to be vulnerable and available at the deepest levels of the soul's ability to communicate.

Emory Cowan, Jr., MDiv, PhD

I would prefer a world where some insights are best conveyed through poetry, and where some experiences can only be captured in words and not numbers.... For such as me, the poetry in this book is a fine way to learn about the human condition.

Art Bohart

Just because Greening dedicated this book to me doesn't mean his drivel is worth reading.

Herbert R. Lochenkopf

If this nonsense is how Greening proposes to fill the void, he has given us one more reason to cultivate emptiness.

Roshi Nada

Dedicated to and blamed on
Herbert R. Lochenkopf, PhD,
my beloved mentor and nemesis.

Table of Contents

Poems

New Poems

Acknowledgements

Many people helped make the original version and this update of *Words Against the Void* possible. I thank the University of the Rockies Press for publishing the original version and granting permission to publish this update. I thank Mary Williams, an early and constant source of encouragement to keep writing. Louis Hoffman has long supported and encouraged my writing of poetry, and helped support the publication of several of my books of poems. Last, I thank Kirk Schneider, Stanley Krippner, Dave Elkins, Art Bohart, and Emory Cowan, who provided support and encouragement in the development of *Words Against the Void.*

Preface
by Emory Cowan

Those of us fortunate enough to know Tom Greening as a professor, therapist, mentor, and/or a friend, will find in these poems wisps of memories of our encounters with him. Tom's gentle persona, his struggles with the nature of human existence, his anguish for the profession of psychology, and his life of authenticity are expressed in these writings. In this body of work, he frames the human condition, our condition, in a way that calls us to reflect, to laugh, and even cry over the meaning and nature of our own existence.

I first met Tom when I was a doctoral student in psychology at Saybrook Graduate School. In those days I felt intimidated by his reputation as a scholar and editor. That quickly dissipated as we began to share our experiences of life and curiosity about people. Occasionally, in those all to brief sessions, he would share his most intimate thoughts and struggles through the poetry he was composing. What a gift from a friend!

Nevertheless, the greatest gift I received from Tom Greening was that of encouragement. Freely given éncouragement, given at a time when he was in the midst of his own grief and pain. He had journeyed and struggled on the same roads of life that I had traveled. For me he became the guide, the brother who called for me to strive for excellence, to commit to service, and to remain true to myself. For me, he embodied Jung's construct and Nouwen's understanding of the *Wounded Healer*.

In these poems, Tom unwraps his wounded self in order to be vulnerable and available at the deepest levels of the soul's ability to communicate. I suspect he will probably take exception to my use of the term, but from my own spiritual tradition, and in the richest since of the word, I believe Tom is a pastor. He is a shepherd, who through his gentle bucolic, yet exacting nature, guides those of us who place ourselves in his care to green pastures and encourages us to drink deeply from still waters.

Foreword
by Art Bohart

So I say to one of my old college professors Heinrich Oubergen, who I had just had the misfortune to run into at lunch at a convention, "Look! I just got this! A book of poetry by Tom Greening!"

"Who," asked Oubergen, "is Tom Greening?"

I said, "You know! The famous existential psychotherapist, former editor of *The Journal of Humanistic Psychology.*"

"Oh yes," asked Oubergen, "*The Journal of Humanistic Psychology.* I vaguely remember that. Sort of a fuzzy, touchy-feely, nonscientific journal, as I recall."

I said, "Well! I don't know about that. It publishes all sorts of articles on an alternative vision of psychology: articles on self-actualization and empathy and peak experiences and dialogue, and meditation and peace, and synergy, and spirituality, and on the evils of psychiatric diagnosis and drugging. It deals with the positive potential in humans."

"What" says Oubergon. "does 'positive potential' mean? Can you define that scientifically? How do you operationalize that? How do you measure it? And what is a *psychologist* doing writing poetry? That is not scientific. He should be spending his time doing experiments. Has he published any research lately on how to condition positive potential? What kinds of significance levels has he found? What do his regression equations look like? His beta weights?"

"Well," I said, "I don't think he's published anything with a regression equation in it. As far as his beta weight, he *is* a chocolate lover, so you never know. But you won't find anything like that in this poetry. This poetry addresses our condition. It talks about what it is to be human. It talks about our experience, about intuition, and being present. It confronts the horrible things people do to one another. It talks about suffering and tragedy. You can learn a lot from reading this poetry. It is insightful."

Oubergon sniffed. "Learn? From poetry? You have to be joking. Poetry has only emotional meaning. If we encourage this kind of thing we might as well send psychology back to the dark ages. If you cannot measure it, it doesn't exist. Here, let me borrow that book. I will write a critique of it."

And so off Oubergon went with the book before I had a chance to protest. I feared I'd never see it again, but, in fact, the next day I saw him and he handed it back to me without a word. I leafed through it and found notes he had written. Next to the following lines he had written "Good!'

> Away with fuzzy-minded thought,
> away with sloppy sentiment--
> Pure science is the one true faith;
> the goal of life is measurement.

But to these next lines:

> Do I belong in such a field?
> Can such a field put up with me?
> When questions such as these grow grim
> for refuge I try poetry.

He had written: "Of course he does not belong in the field. Poetry indeed!"

Oubergon goes on to write:

This fellow clearly has psychological problems of his own. Based on what he writes in this poetry, he is an irresponsible faculty member who shirks his faculty review, writes drivel, whines and snivels, gets on the defensive, and tries to bribe his Dean. Elsewhere he admits that he is a curmudgeon. He also writes as if he is depressed and then says that drugs would help him—something that he is supposedly opposed to! He is not even logical and consistent! And finally, in the following lines, about psychotherapy,

> We wandered in and out the prison gate
> and passed each other in the dark unheard,
> then met at last before it was too late
> and found we did not need to say a word.
> in searching for a better way to care
> without a ray of hope or guiding star
> the only way to get from here to there
> is learning how to be the place we are.

he wanders all over the place instead of providing a sound treatment plan based on the use of specific, empirically validated procedures. No wonder all he can offer is to "learn how to be the place you are." He doesn't know how to be helpful in any other way.

Oubergon concludes that Greening could probably use a dose of good therapy himself to set his thinking right.

I was dismayed. I couldn't believe that Oubergon had taken Greening's poetry seriously, as if he really thought that he was in favor of drugging himself (with other than chocolate), or that he was seriously depressed, or curmudgeonly (well, maybe a bit curmudgeonly), or opposed to social change. Oubergen didn't seem to realize that Greening was using a device in his poetry that the songwriter Randy Newman is famous for, called the "unreliable narrator" (according to my favorite reference source, Wikipedia). That is where the narrator of the song, or poem, adopts a persona in order to satirize it. For instance, in Randy Newman's song "Political Science," the narrator is a character who is dismayed at how people in other parts of the world hate the United States, and suggests that we "drop the big one" on them. But we don't really believe that Randy Newman is advocating dropping the big one.

Of course, as I thought this to myself, I realized that as soon as I explained this, Greening would redouble his efforts at satire and become even more ironic. I could even imagine a poem where he adopts the persona of an unreliable narrator talking about being an unreliable narrator!

For purposes of intellectual integrity here, I must disclose that I am, however, committed to believing that Greening's poetry is ironic. There is a poem about me in this collection. It is about my "Neglected Works of Arthur Bohart," a title I have proposed for a collection of the many articles that I have published but which no one, as far as I can tell, has ever read. I am currently looking for a publisher. In the poem, Greening concludes that I am a "putz." Clearly he must be being ironic.

As far as Greening's insights into psychotherapy and into the human condition, I realized that Oubergon would never understand them. I thought about writing a reply, but realized it would be fruitless. Someone as literal as Oubergon would never grasp the insights of Greening's poetry. Nor its humor. I decided to leave Oubergon to his world of operational definitions and belief only in things that could be measured.

For me, I would prefer a world where some insights are best conveyed through poetry, and where some experiences can only be captured in words and not numbers, although I am not opposed to numbers. For such as me, the poetry in this book is a fine way to learn about the human condition.

Introduction to *Words Against the Void*
By Louis Hoffman

Tom Greening is the most prolific poet I have ever met. On several occasions, I participated in email exchanges with Tom where his responses, which came back mere minutes after the last email I sent, were all in poetry. At conferences, Tom will often write poetic responses to the presentation that summarize and advance the dialogue. He participates in listserv conversations with poetry that flows with the conversation. Over time, I have wondered if Tom has evolved to think in poetry!

In the quantity of poetry produced and shared by Tom, some miss the depth woven throughout his poems. While his poems are enjoyable to read, it would be a great loss to mistake them for mere entertainment. With each poem, the reader is invited to go deeper and look at the nature of being human and living in the contemporary world. As you read, or re-read, *Words Against the Void,* my encouragement is to let the poems take you deeper. Meditate on the meanings and see what you can learn from them about the human condition.

One of the foundations of existential psychology is the commitment to look at the world honestly with all its stark realities. When interviewed as part of Trent Claypool's (2010) dissertation, *On Becoming an Existential Therapist: The Journeys of Contemporary Leaders*, Tom spoke profoundly to this topic:

> I finally went to a concentration camp for the first time in my life last August... I wanted to do that, and am glad I did. It was a very powerful experience. It sort of felt like paying one's existential dues... That if you are going to be alive in the 20th century or 21st century, that you are going to claim to be alive and had lived in that time, then what should you be aware of, or in touch with? (p. 82)

Reading Tom's poetry is one way of paying one's existential dues. Through the poems, one is confronted with the difficult realities of the world today. In "Managed Care," one could easily read this as a poem poking fun at the managed care system. Yet, this poem does more than poking fun: It shows the absurdity of the philosophical foundations of the managed care system.

> What medicine will cool our feverish brow?
> What X-rays show us where our souls are cracked?
> What treatment plan will clearly tell us how
> to find at last the love we've always lacked?

In poetic form, Tom provides a penetrating critique of the medical model in psychotherapy and, with great conservation of words, illustrates its limitations and failures.

As a therapist, I am aware that we cannot just throw our clients into the void and stark realities of the world. First, it is necessary to provide for some security or foundation. Greening provides a parallel to this in his poetry. The soothing rhymes and frequent humor of Tom's poems provide a comforting balance to the sometimes despairing topics he engages. The poems soothe as they invite one to grab a flashlight and go spelunking into the dark caverns of humanity.

While many of the poems explore social conditions, such as managed care and the pharmaceutical industry, others guide the reader into engaging their own soul, such as in "No Time to Feel":

> and yet at times I lie awake
> obsessed by sudden doubt—
> I worry that I'm just a fool
> and somehow missing out.
> I do not hope to really live
> but merely to survive,
> but will I mourn when I'm near death
> not having been alive?

Much like reading Camus, Tom's poems invite the reader to engage in self-reflection and think deeply about one's own life and decisions. His poems invite us to live, and to live with greater awareness, engagement, and openness.

It would be a great disservice to write an introduction to a book of Tom's poems without mentioning the frequent theme of self-deprecation, which has, at times, brought fear and concern to his friends. In "My (Failed) Search for Authenticity," Tom writes:

> My failed attempts have forced me to agree:
> authentic presence is too much for me.
> Because I know I can't escape my fetters
> I'll leave the quest for freedom to my betters.
> The joints of my ontology are creaking,
> so now an inauthentic life I'm seeking.

Some readers may be caught off guard by poems that seem strongly self-critical, yet if one gets caught up in concern about Tom's suffering the point of the poem will be missed.

The self-depreciating poems are among Tom's most powerful and they profoundly illustrate the existential nature of his writing. While there is an authenticity in these poems, it is not in the revelation of desperation or despair, but in the general openness to one's failures and limitations. In contemporary society, people are so concerned with how people perceive them that they often hide any sign of weakness or flaw. This is notably evident in the contemporary world of politics where an acknowledgement of weakness or mistake can quickly end one's career. Tom, instead, recognizes that human limitation and failure are inherent in the human condition. To deny one's failure is to deny oneself and limit the ability to which one can truly experience self-acceptance:

> It could be argued from an existential perspective the
> therapist' s acceptance of the client, and the client' s self-
> acceptance, is deeper if it is inclusive of the negative,
> hostile, and aggressive feelings. It is easier to accept one's

> feeling of love and appreciation for others than to accept the more negative and conflicted aspects of the person. (Hoffman, Lopez, & Moats, 2013, p. 14)

Through looking more deeply at one's failures, one opens to their potentials, including a deeper potential for self-compassion and acceptance.

Yet, to read Tom's self-deprecating poems as being about self-disclosure misses the point. Often, they are not accurate self-disclosure but rather exaggerations intended to prompt a reflective process. I read each of these poems as an invitation to look honestly at myself and my context in this world.

In the Revised and Updated Edition to *Words Against the Void*, over 25 new poems were added. These new poems were carefully selected to fit with the general theme of the book while engaging issues in contemporary culture and Tom's own life. In recent years, Tom has written extensively about the aging process, including his book *Poems For and About Elders* (Revised and Updated Edition). Several new poems fit thematically with his poems about the aging process.

In several new poems, Tom addresses themes that continue from the original volume through critiquing the new *Diagnostic and Statistical Manual of Mental Disorders, Fifth Edition* ("DSM Whatever") as well as the medical model in therapy and the pharmaceutical industry ("Blame Our Brains," "Confessions of a Troll," and "Side Effects"). For most of his career, Tom has been a strong advocate for humanizing the field of mental health through his long-time leadership in humanistic psychology, his teaching at Saybrook University, his involvement in professional organizations, and serving as editor of the *Journal of Humanistic Psychology*. For Tom, the medicalization of psychology is not just a threat to his profession, but it is an existential threat. He is deeply aware of the suffering and harm caused by treating clients as patients, and treating people as objects.

Shifting to a more profound critique of contemporary culture, "Dog's Story" is a challenging poem. When Tom originally proposed including this poem, I was resistant. Particularly as a dog lover, I found this poem too painful to read. I wanted to put it away and forget about it. The strong discomfort I experienced in reading this poem prevented me from seeing the deeper meaning. The story of this poem is of animal cruelty—torturing and killing a dog. What deeper meaning could this have?

As I reflected upon this question, a Bruce Springsteen song came to mind. In Springsteen's song, "Nebraska," he tells a story based upon true events of two teenagers who went on a killing spree for no apparent reason. At the end of the song, Springsteen (1982) sings,

> They declare me unfit to live
> Said into that great void my soul'd be hurled
> They wanted to know why I did what I did
> Well, sir, I guess there's just a meanness in this world

I am writing this introduction in early 2017 when the "meanness in this world" is in full display. It is easy to want to pretend this does not exist, that the world is a better place than it is. It is easy to want to believe that we do not need to be aware of the hate and the atrocities occurring in the world. Although we can easily get overloaded with reality in the 21st century and it is healthy to limit our consumption of reality at times, a certain degree is necessary to be responsible citizens of the world as well as the country and community in which we live. And sometimes, as difficult as it is to bear, we need to be aware that dogs and people are being tortured and killed, and not just by "the enemy."

Fortunately, Tom does not leave us with this stark facing of reality thrust upon the reader. He continues his analysis through other new poems. In "Our Legacy" he speaks about our proclivity to war and violence, questioning if this is what we want our legacy as the human race to be:

> Survey all human history–
> Is blindness our main legacy?

While this still may seem bleak, it is important to go beyond the surface of the words. The poem, through calling us on our blindness, encourages us to awaken while we still have time to save our legacy from one that, at times, seems destined toward extinction.

In the final two poems, Tom leads us more directly to hope. In "Sitting with Dog," Tom reflects on writing a poem while his dog impatiently waits for him to finish and return his attention to more important things:

> But my attempt to write this poem
> has disturbed him,
> so I will stop and go back to just sitting,
> breathing in rhythm with my nuzzling comrade
> on our last journey.

While Tom's poetry is important, he recognizes that what is truly important is relationship. When embarking on one's last journey, this reality becomes more evident. In the end his dog had it right, and Tom listened.

The collection concludes with "A Poet's Plea," which calls for an ending of war and return to poetry and literature. Maybe, just maybe, if we focused more on the depths of meaning that can be found in the arts instead of on power, control, and ego, we would discover that poetry and literature are not just alternatives to war, but preventive treatment:

> Please postpone wars when're you can,
> perhaps impose a stringent ban
> on bombing people whom we need
> our precious poetry to read.

I want to conclude with a few personal reflections on my friend and colleague, Tom Greening. It has been over 10-years since I first met my friend. After hearing many stories about Tom from Emory Cowan, I was intrigued to get to know Tom better when we met. We quickly discovered that we shared many common loves: poetry, dogs, and existential psychology.

I long had wondered why Tom, who had given so much to the field of psychology, particularly humanistic psychology, was not better recognized and known for his many contributions. He was the editor of the *Journal of Humanistic Psychology* for 35-years and, along with Stanley Krippner, one of the longest serving faculty members at Saybrook University, the premiere university in the world for existential-humanistic psychology. It is a shame that Tom has not been more celebrated for his leadership and contributions.

Tom practiced psychotherapy for over 50-years in the same office where he began his private practice with James F. T. Bugental the same year in which Rollo May's *Existence* was published (1958). With Bugental, they brought May to Los Angeles for a training seminar. These events shaped the future of humanistic psychology and the development of existential-humanistic psychotherapy.

Tom was instrumental in the early development of Saybrook University (originally the Humanistic Psychology Institute), serving on the board and as a faculty member. Over the years, he taught, mentored, and supervised many who would become leaders in the humanistic and existential psychology movements in the United States. Yet, Tom did not seek out the limelight. Instead, he humbly served and was happy to support others to become better recognized than he was.

In my years in the field of psychology, I have watched many people ascend to and seek leadership roles. There are those who seek board roles, faculty appointments, and other leadership roles with a sense of entitlement or solely for the purpose of advancing their career. Others recognize that these are, at their heart, service roles. As service roles, there is a sacred quality to them that needs to be honored. Those who recognize this as opposed to self-serving goals are almost without fail the best leaders. When I was first encouraged to run for president of the

Society for Humanistic Psychology, I was very reticent. I remember my friend, Dave Elkins, saying that this reticence maybe was a sign that I was ready and could serve well in the role. Few people embody this lesson as well as Tom. He has lived a life of service that has impacted many, many lives. His leadership roles and accolades were not pursed for any self-aggrandizement, but out of a deep commitment to his students, his peers, and the field.

The impact that Tom has had on the field of humanistic and existential psychology should not be forgotten or underestimated. It has been profound. It is hard to imagine that these fields would be where they are today without him.

Personally, I feel deeply indebted to Tom for many reasons. I am indebted for what he has given in service to fields of humanistic and existential psychology that I love. I am indebted for his commitment to the value of poetry in the psychological realm, which helped empower me to integrate poetry into my work as a professor and psychologist. But mostly, I am appreciative of the years I have served with Tom as a colleague and friend. I know this relationship has deeply blessed me and this I always will carry proudly with me.

Thank you, Tom, for your poetry, your service, your friendship, and your heart.

References

Claypool., T. (2010). *On becoming an existential therapist: The journeys of contemporary leaders.* Retrieved from ProQuest database (UMI 3412340).

Hoffman, L., Lopez, A., & Moats, M. (2013). Humanistic psychology and self-acceptance. In M. Bernard (Ed.), *The strength of self-acceptance: Theory, research, and practice* (pp. 3-17). New York: NY: Springer.

Springsteen, B. (1982). Nebraska [Recorded by Bruce Springsteen]. On *Nebraska* [CD]. United States: Columbia.

Poems

Never doubt that a small group of thoughtful,
committed citizens can
change the world. Indeed, it is
the only thing that ever has.
   Margaret Mead

Never doubt that a small group of thoughtless,
demented citizens can
mess up the world. Indeed, it is the only thing that
you can always count on.
   Tom Greening

FREEDOM vs. DETERMINISM

Just reacting? Freely striving?
Blindly driven? Wisely driving?
Who's the rider? Who's the horse?
Who's in charge? Who charts the course?
Sort your data, choose your theory,
Argue concepts 'til you're weary.
Psychologize until you die--
While we argue, life goes by.

INTUITION

Here's a challenge and a mission--
developing our intuition.
We need more freedom from the known
and must not count on thought alone.
No matter how astute we are
our reason takes us just so far
and cannot help us to discern
the other ways we need to learn.
Instead of logic and precision
we also need a deeper vision,
ways to think in metaphor
and draw upon unconscious lore.
But here I sit, trapped in my mind,
and do not know if I can find
a way to shake the evil curse
that makes me write such stilted verse.

KIERKEGAARD'S PARADOX

Some more of that, some more of this—
thus will I some day savor bliss.
Or should I abjure everything,
give up the stuff to which I cling
so I can set my poor soul free
and dwell in perfect poverty?
Some days I gain, some days I lose—
I never know which one to choose—
when to constrict, when to expand—
that's what I cannot understand.
And thus I swing from pole to pole,
confused about my proper goal,
but in the process try to be
alive more existentially.

NIGHT JOURNEY

As I perused the gloomy paper trail
that marked this patient's lengthy fall from grace
I realized that I would also fail
and write him off as just a hopeless case
unless I sprung us both out of our trap
and met him in a place we'd never been.
But for this pathless journey there's no map,
and just a rusty gyroscope within.
We wandered in and out the prison gate
and passed each other in the dark unheard,
then met at last before it was too late
and found we did not need to say a word.
In searching for a better way to care
without a ray of hope or guiding star,
the only way to get from here to there,
is learning how to be the place we are.

NO TIME TO FEEL

The way that I've arranged my life,
I've left no time to feel.
This anesthetic works so well
I never do reveal
my feelings even to myself
or to those close to me.
By keeping busy all the time
I act like I am free,
and if I have some time to spare
I fill it up real fast,
and pray this numbing sedative
is somehow going to last.
When nosey people question me
I hasten to explain
this is my plan to get through life
by minimizing pain,
and yet at times I lie awake
obsessed by sudden doubt—
I worry that I'm just a fool
and somehow missing out.
I do not hope to really live
but merely to survive,
but will I mourn when I'm near death
not having been alive?

FLIGHT FROM BEING

I try to be quite deferential
toward colleagues who are existential.
Their vision is profound and deep
while I am always half asleep.
I cannot face contingency
and sheer existence frightens me.
I constantly am panicked, fleeing
from all the challenges of being.
I stumble through befuddled days
beleaguered by a vague malaise.
The search for authenticity
is far beyond a dolt like me--
I much prefer duplicity.
Commitment just repulses me,
but I am sure I will be fine
if I can hide from crass Dasein.

PSYCHOLOGY

As I came into consciousness
there was a war where millions died,
and even when frail peace broke out
life's anguish left me horrified.

I worked in mental hospitals,
construction jobs and factories;
I traveled where the war had been
and contemplated tragedies.

Perplexed by what I'd seen of life,
appalled by so much misery,
I sought to understand the cause
and thought I'd try psychology.

I hoped I'd find some people there
who cared about the human soul,
but learned instead it was our job
to do "prediction and control."

And sure enough, some governments
have found psychologists can aid
in customizing torture skills,
a job for which they're amply paid.

Not all psychology, thank God,
is used for purposes so cruel,
but much of what it's all about
is tailored to a basic rule:

Whatever does in fact exist
exists in some precise amount,
and so our task is to devise
precision tools with which to count.

Away with fuzzy-minded thought,
away with sloppy sentiment--
Pure science is the one true faith;
the goal of life is measurement.

Do I belong in such a field?
Can such a field put up with me?
When questions such as these grow grim
for refuge I try poetry.

A SINGLE CASE STUDY

I am an anomalous surge,
a bioelectromagnetic burst.
Study me with EEG topographic mapping
(a great advance over phrenology),
ferret out my subtle energies,
record the markers of my emotion,
sift my positive and negative ions
for signs of virtue,
and measure the build-up and collapse
of my electric dipoles
while I indulge my mood swings.
I'll gulp down any placebo,
ignorant as I am of
psychopharmacology.
When you've done with
the biofeedback stress profiling
please give me copies of the charts and graphs
to frame and hang over the fireplace
so on cold nights when my current flickers
I can remember who I am.

LOVE THE CROW

There is nothing in any religion
That teaches us to love the pigeon
  - Ogden Nash

Too bad for pigeons--this I know:
God wants us all to love the crow.
He may look black and sinister,
but so does my own minister.

WEARY OF THEORY

Behaviorists in all their wisdom
feel it isn't worth their work
to explore the human psyche,
full of mystery and murk.

They would rather study action,
focus on behavior seen,
not unseen, unseemly insides,
motives, meanings Byzantine.

Humanists, their fuzzy colleagues,
have a very different goal:
They would elevate the species
and affirm the human soul.

Then there's existentialism,
focused on our finitude,
angst, contingency and freedom,
all with dread of death imbued.

Psychoanalytic pundits
eruditely analyze
our fixations and resistance,
thus attempting to be wise.

Cognitive behavior theorists
study how we learn and think.
I grow weary of these theories—
too much thought drives me to drink.

I have searched such books for wisdom,
but it's mostly been in vain,
so I merely write these verses,
hoping thus to entertain.

REQUEST

For all these years I've not been here
because I have a chronic fear
that being in the present tense
would strip me of my last defense
against the terror known as "life,"
which I have found to be too rife
with anguish, heartbreak and despair
for any feeling soul to bear.
Thus I have kept myself apart,
pretended that I have no heart,
avoided being too awake,
and searched for ways that I could fake
a pseudo-personality
concealed in much banality
to deftly substitute in lieu
of really being here with you.
I've gotten very good at this,
and only dimly do I miss
the warmth that other people feel
who have the courage to be real.
I think my way of life is best,
and so I make this firm request:
Don't wake me up, don't make me see
my triumph is a tragedy.

LAPSED EXISTENTIALIST

I must confess that I've become annoyed
by seeing naught about me but the void,
and so I clutch and cling to lots of stuff
but never seem to gather quite enough.
How many loves and dollars will it take
to fill me up and my grim thirsting slake?
This question occupies each waking hour,
and all the while my mood grows dark and dour.
I wish this could be called philosophy,
yet fear it's just a dreary travesty.
I'd hoped that for my courage I'd be known,
but ended up a dreary rhyming drone.
I'm nothing but a boring pessimist,
a lapsed and defrocked existentialist.

VONNEGUT'S VISION

"I want to stay as close to the edge as I can without going over. Out
on the edge you see all kinds of things you can't see from the center."
   - Kurt Vonnegut

I'm sitting out here on the ledge,
sitting almost at the edge,
but what I see is quite unclear
and all I feel is lots of fear.
Kurt Vonnegut had two good eyes
and saw through all the sham and lies.
I just cower petrified,
by illusions mystified.
Please, somebody rescue me—
I cannot live heroically.
Instead of insights new, profound,
I long to tread familiar ground.
If humankind can be set free
it will not be by such as me.

ACROPHOBIA

"You've got to jump off cliffs all the time
and build your wings on the way down."
  - Ray Bradbury

Never having bravely jumped,
I must admit that I am stumped.
I don't know how to build a wing
and am afraid of everything.
I'd panic, shriek, and tremble if
I found myself atop a cliff.
I'd quiver, quake, and quickly run,
'cause that's not my idea of fun.
At least I do not make a fuss
like that pretentious Icarus.
I'm cowardly confessing that
I live my life down where it's flat,
admitting with a mournful sigh,
I'm terrified of getting high.

MY (FAILED) SEARCH FOR AUTHENTICITY

I've always had the secret, haunting fear
that my essential Self will disappear.
For years I've spewed much existential blather,
but I confess that now I'd really rather
give up my ranting over love and will
and let my weary mind at last be still.
I must admit I've found it very hard
to understand the thought of Kierkegaard.
We never seem to find ourselves agreeing
on what it is that constitutes our Being.
I hope you will forgive these angst-full lapses
as products of my over-worked synapses.
As I survey the shambles of my brain
I see Dasein and meaning on the wane,
while idle chatter rattles all day long
too seldom interrupted by a song.
My failed attempts have forced me to agree:
authentic presence is too much for me.
Because I know I can't escape my fetters
I'll leave the quest for freedom to my betters.
The joints of my ontology are creaking,
so now an inauthentic life I'm seeking.

ABSENCE

When my encounters get too deep
I find I tend to fall asleep.
I don't know what it is could make
me really want to stay awake.

Life being what it is these days
it never ceases to amaze
me that some folk can stay alert
and run the risk of being hurt.

So I doze off, and feel secure
and seldom have I felt the lure
of being present in my life
and risking consciousness and strife.

Don't take this as a rude affront–
I'm sorry if I seem too blunt.
I beg you for your sympathy–
I'm having trouble being me.

SALVATION LOST

When there's no god around
I'm really not annoyed,
because I find my peace
in staring at the void.

I've seen no gods today–
I don't know where they are.
Perhaps they don't exist–
so near and yet so far!

When I have lost my way
I feel a healing grace
in finding I'm alone
in empty, pristine space.

But I can't stand that long–
I'll fill it up with junk.
I'll find some new beliefs
and end up in a funk.

FEAR OF LIGHT

"When you realize that everything is light, you are enlightened."
   - Anonymous spiritual teacher

When I'm assured that everything is light
it really gives me a horrific fright,
for I prefer to shoot up in the dark
and cravenly evade the local narc.

I quaver, quake, and get extremely frightened
when I meet folks who claim to be enlightened.
I run and hide behind the nearest idol
and pray my fears won't make me suicidal.

If dawn should come and catch me unawares
I fear it will expose my woes and cares.
I'll close my eyes and hope I'll never see
a glimpse of what some call reality

AWARENESS

The Spring, 1988 issue of *ReVision* contained an article by Albert Hofmann, the discoverer of LSD and former director of research of Sandoz Pharmaceutical Laboratories, entitled "The Transmitter-Receiver Concept of Reality" discussing our relationship to what we call "reality." The following poem was written in response to that article.

Although I'm aging,
my retinas still see
in living color
a few electromagnetic waves,
but just those
from .4 to .7 millimicrons—
that is, from what we call red
to what we call blue.
And, I'm happy to say,
my tympanic membranes
still hear a few waves
amidst the acoustical ocean.
Some we call Bach.
I can't explain how I taste
certain molecular structures,
but I do,
and so it is with touch and smell.
Thus I keep in contact
with what we call reality,
and I have a lot of opinions about it.
My problem is
I know I'm missing out
on most of the waves.
Why should bees see more,
dogs smell more,
bats hear more?
And even they are missing
most of the show.
Why plunk down
such a small receiver

in the midst of this symphony?
When I die
do I get to hear it all?

MY SYNAPSES

Why do I have these wild relapses?
I blame them on my sick synapses.
My brain lacks neural density
resulting in sub par plasticity.
With neurons frayed, flawed, and deficient
my coping skills are insufficient.
That's why I want to kiss and hug
the doc who gives me some new drug
each month and blithely reassures me
this one at last will surely cure me.

CURE

In his review of a book by Marty Jezer, *Abbie Hoffman: American
Rebel* in the January 13, 1993 *Los Angeles Times,* Jonathan Kirsch
claims that Abbie died "the victim of a mental illness that may have
prompted his many pranks in the first place," and describes him as
suffering from "bipolar disorder." Thus, the political activist who was
once Abraham Maslow's student and the court jester of the
counterculture is explained away by the medical model. I must
confess that I suffer from the same disease. But there is a cure, as the
following poem reveals.

I have a vexing problem with
a dread disease that is no myth.
I get upset by world events,
by suffering and sad laments,
by children starving in the east
while richer folk carouse and feast.
Genetically I am impaired
and far too often have despaired
about our inhumanity,
thus showing my insanity.
My saner friends don't sadly dwell
on how the earth resembles hell.
Their biochemistry is fine,
while mine is more like turpentine.
Their neurons fire the way they should,
while I have never understood
the way the world is organized,
and so I always am surprised
by horrors others take in stride,
by innocence still crucified.
While cheerful folk feel they are blessed,
I'm pathologically depressed.
But there is hope, my doctor swears,
new wonder drugs will ease my cares.
He'll fix my too empathic brain,
he'll make my sick synapses sane.

My mental illness can be cured
and all the anguish I've endured
will no more plague my deranged head,
and my compassion will be dead.

BRAIN CHEMISTRY

Up in my head there's quite a stew--
My brain with chemicals is rife.
There's something that I wish I knew:
Do neuropeptides run my life?

I'm quite confused and plagued by doubt.
These clever drugs and their receptors,
If they're not neatly sorted out,
Will make us all into their debtors.

To be or not to be, and who?
I don't know where my self is at.
Of truth I haven't got a clue--
Can neuropeptides tell me that?

I'll struggle on, though I'm a mess,
Pretending I am not insane.
My soul cries out, I must confess,
For chemistry to fix my brain.

I barely have survived thus far
Unmedicated falls from grace.
If this is what we really are,
Can drugs redeem the human race?

MANAGED CARE

Provide, provide some balm to ease our pain,
bestow on us an angel's healing grace,
an ample dose of Camus or Coltrane,
an antidote to stop our lemming's race.

What's covered and what claims will be denied?
Lear's madness now infects the entire race.
Prescribe a cure to save the old man's pride,
dispense a drug to save us from disgrace.

What medicine will cool our feverish brow?
What X-rays show us where our souls are cracked?
What treatment plan will clearly tell us how
to find at last the love we've always lacked?

Third party payors tightly hold the purse,
and terror grips us in our restless sleep.
Who knows what charges they will reimburse?
Salvation on this earth does not come cheap.

Tight economic limits rule the day,
the bureaucrats will ascertain the price
of rescuing we sheep who've gone astray,
and short-term therapy must now suffice.

Be generous, while you contain the cost--
Life's harder than we ever realized.
We're floundering, our ark is nearly lost--
Be merciful, if that is authorized.

MATTER

"We have learned that matter is weird stuff."
  - Physicist F. J. Dyson in *Infinite in All Directions*.
    Harper & Row, 1988, p.8

As if I weren't upset enough,
I now am told I'm made of stuff
a physicist declares is weird,
exactly what I've always feared.

My mother was no scientist,
but she would endlessly insist
on this same fact about my core,
which did not make my spirits soar.

I don't believe these physicists,
'cause something deep in me resists,
and still believes there is a God
who only made me slightly odd.

POSTMODERN PRAYER

"So the constructivists and their ilk--and, as we will see, it is a pretty big ilk--are permitted to go more or less freely about their heretical business."
  - Walter Truett Anderson, *Reality Isn't What It Used To Be*. Harper & Row, 1990, page xii.

Constructivists and their sick ilk
are clearly plotting ways to bilk
me out of my reality,
at least it seems that way to me.
Of course, it's possible I'm wrong—
my grasp on truth is not too strong,
in which case I'm just one of them,
the foes I eagerly condemn.
I'm not at home on their wild range
with new ideas that are so strange.
I want some truth that's hard as rock—
don't tell me that it's just a crock.

PROBLEM GOD

My stupid god just slurs and mumbles,
and mostly he ignores my grumbles.
You'd think a god would have good diction
and be conversant with great fiction.
He hasn't read the classic books
and claims philosophers are schnooks.
I bet this guy is an imposter
and never in me faith will foster.
He loafs in heaven looking glum
and I've concluded he's plain dumb.
I've got to find another one
who, if not smart, at least is fun.

NIETZSCHE WAS WRONG

Nietzsche was wrong,
seriously wrong,
when he claimed, "God is dead."
We should be so lucky!
The old fart is more alive
than you and I,
and having a really bad trip
on acid he got cheap
from Lucifer.
He'll come down eventually
and go back to his old ways
as an absentee slumlord,
not dead,
but a deadbeat.
It's up to us to get him into
some kind of 12-step rehab program,
but that first step may be
more than he can take.

RESEARCH

Psychological research would be easier,
more precise, if God were not
a confounding variable.
I was taught, "If something exists
it exists in some quantity
and can be measured."
I still have the micrometer
my grandfather used working as a steel roller,
and the diary in which he recorded
the date of my mother's birth, her gender,
but not her name,
or the dimensions of his faith.
The thickness of steel and skin
surrenders to our calipers,
but God is an enraged whale
who lunges at our leaking boat,
then plunges down and down,
the harpoon fifty centimeters deep
in his mortal flesh,
the rope (an inch thick)
tangled around our legs
dragging us behind him.

ALTERNATIVE

Most of your waking life
will be spent, one way or another,
worrying about your worth as a person.
Why don't you just make something up,
and right off the bat
be done with the whole problem?
There must be better things to do
than fret about your relative merit
in the universe.
You could, for example,
blow clouds around the sky
to the delight of small children.

FUSSY MIND

Alas, sometimes my mind grows dark and dirty
And even can think ill of Krishnamurti.
But Buddha never said we must be saintly,
Just conscious of what is, however faintly.
So when I fuss about my guru's sex life,
Or worry how he'll make out in the next life,
I sit until my eager ego's absent,
So I can twitch in the eternal present.

FEAR OF DRUGS

Here's my complaint, my sad lament
when asked to give my signed consent
to let them drug me with their pills
for all my existential ills:

Their chemical surcease appeals
to one like me who sadly feels
that life is full of woe and stress,
whose synapses are quite a mess.

But wait, this is my only brain,
and when its monsters have been slain
or maybe only lulled a bit,
will I be left with any wit?

The doctors claim they know a lot,
but their opinions have been bought.
When they have cured me of my cares,
I fear my brain will be like theirs.

NOT GUILTY

If you believe in the insanity defense
then you've got to exonerate Kissinger
and most foreign policy makers
who valiantly struggle with the handicap
of a chemical imbalance
resulting from an inherited genetic flaw.
They are not bad men, just sick,
and not to be held responsible.
Their sister, Andrea Yates,
is equally afflicted,
but killed fewer children.
In the future, medication
may bring us all peace.
These people do the best they can
in an equally mad world,
and I suspect that Lewis Carroll
is secretly behind it all.

EMPIRICALLY VALIDATED PSYCHOTHERAPY

What works in psychotherapy?
That's far beyond the likes of me.
I've only practiced fifty years,
and still am plagued by doubts and fears.
I muddle on and try my best
to aid my clients in their quest
for ways of being more alive,
somehow in spite of all to thrive.
I wish I knew the right technique
to give them more of what they seek.
The mystery of change persists
unsolved by dogged scientists.
I hope that they will soon impart
quick ways to heal a broken heart.
My efforts stagger, balk, and lurch
unguided by precise research
to tell me how to ease life's pains,
and thus flawed intuition reigns.
Pray science soon will guarantee
sure cures for human misery,
but meanwhile I'll do what I can
without a validated plan.

MY GENES

I'm daily growing more frenetic
in hopes my problems are genetic
for then they won't be blamed on me
and I can get more sympathy.
I'm grateful to each scientist
who helps me righteously insist
that I'd be perfect were it not
for those flawed genes I somehow got.
There's ample reason to suppose
those faulty genes cause all my woes
and I myself am innocent
of sins and crimes I can't prevent.
Thus sadly I can just lament
this biologic accident
and go about my errant ways
quite freely in a guilt-free daze.

PAXIL IN PREGNANCY

*The FDA said the benefits of the drug to the
mother may outweigh the risk to the fetus.*

The drugs I take are good for me,
and so I'm really glad to see
that Paxil cheers up pregnant chicks.
It's just the thing to quickly fix
depression and a tendency
to play upon our sympathy.
Those birth defects are balanced by
less tendency to bitch and cry.
We men can all attest that it's
replete with rosy benefits.
I hope the stodgy FDA
will see it in this upbeat way.

APOLOGETIC

Why am I always so apologetic?
I fear I have a flaw that is genetic
that makes me often drastically dyspeptic
or cycle into being quite frenetic.

My so-called friends say I am just pathetic
disturbed, deranged, and not at all noetic,
and that makes me grow wildly apoplectic,
so then they claim I'm borderline psychotic.

In hopes they will become more sympathetic
I'm trying to stop acting so neurotic.
My doctor has prescribed a neuroleptic.
but I'd prefer a cure that's more poetic.

FUSION

I'm happy with my dear delusion
that I'll be saved by love as fusion.
Beset by my primeval urge
I know that only if I merge
will I transcend my lonely plight
and somehow make it through the night.
I can't face life all on my own--
Just thinking of it makes me groan.
My therapist claims she is sure
that I'm becoming more mature,
but meanwhile lets me take a nap
curled up securely in her lap.

VOLUNTARY ADMISSION

Please hear my wail, my sad lament:
I never gave informed consent.
They lied to me and fed me crap
and now I'm caught in their cruel trap.
They ominously said they'll "treat" me,
which really means they will defeat me.
Long-term effects will last for years
and sorely aggravate my fears.
They give me pills to cool me out
and never leave the slightest doubt
that absent any humane care
I'm on a diet of despair.

DEPRESSION CURED

I'm grateful to the docs who now reveal
that my depression is not fake—it's real.
It does not stem from how I live my life
or whether I'm bummed out by human strife.
I must admit that I am truly pleased
to learn it's caused by tissue that's diseased.
No longer need I seek the source within
or in the world so overrun with sin.
A wonder drug will fix each flawed synapse
and never will I fear a grim relapse.

ELECTROSHOCK

Electroshock will turn you on--
all your troubles soon be gone.
Bless that electricity--
brings you fine felicity.
Burdened down with woe and sin,
want to fix the mood you're in?
Jolt your sad soul out of hock--
thank God for electroshock!
(Do not ask him to explain
what it does to your poor brain.)

OUR BEST HOPE

There are some foolish folks who think
we do not teeter on the brink.
It is my goal to do research
that serves to sully and besmirch
those happy dolts who stir my bile
each time they dare to laugh or smile.
How can they claim to savor life
with all its horror, slaughter, strife?
I'll prove existence is unfair
and our best hope lies in despair.

CARPE DIEM?

Why is it that I never see 'em,
those folks who proclaim, "Carpe Diem"?
They happily indulge in revels
while I fight off my inner devils.
They seize each day and grasp at pleasures
while I take cautionary measures.
They're living lives of sheer delight
while I consider if I might
stroll briefly in the summer sun
without offending anyone.
Well, life is short, and soon it's done,
so why waste time in having fun?

MENTAL ILLNESS (SIC)

There is one thing that I abhor:
a badly misused metaphor,
thus I have really had my fill
of being told my mind is "ill,"
and do not tell me that my brain
is ganz vermischt and quite insane.
Our flesh gets sick, and minds get screwy,
as you can see in Uncle Louie.
Some thoughts, of course, can be bizarre:
Poor Louie thinks that he's the Czar.
But I get violent perforce
if you mix levels of discourse.
Please use our language as permitted
or I'll have miscreants committed.

SANE

I know this must sound bizarrely inane—
but now I'm at last synthetically sane.
The pills that I take are making me calm,
providing each day a life-saving balm.
There's some that prevent my being a creep,
and some of them help me drift off to sleep.
Without my pink pills who knows what I'd do?
And when pink pills fail I've some that are blue.
This medicine cures my symptoms quite fast—
my lunatic trips are safely long past.
One problem remains: I doze and I nod
and wake with a start convinced I am God.

SANER THAN THOU

Some people find it odd and strange
that I lack any wish to change.
I'm perfect just the way I am,
and frankly I don't give a damn
about the fact that some folks grow,
because by now you all should know
that I've evolved remarkably
and have no need for therapy.
Perhaps you'd like to ask me how
I got to be more sane than Thou.

PSYCHIATRIC SLAVERY

Written in response to Thomas Szasz's
Coercion as Cure: A Critical History of Psychiatry

A pox on psychiatric slavery--
bad medicine's own brand of knavery.
It's time we ceased consorting with
this quaint profession based on myth.
I'm tired of trying to explain
the mind is different from the brain.
A foolishness that I abhor
is mixing fact with metaphor:
A "mental illness" can't exist
no matter what those docs insist.
I rant and rave and beg them, please:
be clear about what is disease.
The mind has thoughts, the brain is flesh
in New York, Rome or Marrakech,
and one thing sure is indisputable:
all cures need not be pharmaceutical.

OUR MEDICATED ARMY

Results from studies indicate
that we should amply medicate
our soldiers fighting this good war,
and thus inure them to the gore
so they will calm down well before
they all go bonkers and implore
our government to end this mess
that causes them such dreadful stress.
In fact, let's drug the rest of us
so we can be oblivious.

CHOICE?

It's time to celebrate, rejoice!
I've found out that I have a choice!
I can go on just being me,
submitting to my destiny
as victim, loser, fool, or dolt,
or else creatively revolt.
Let's see, what do I want to be?
I'd like to live responsibly
and help our troubled government
be led by a wise president.
It's time to bounce back from disgrace:
Let's help Obama win the race!

Written for the conference "Building Truth – Building Trust" Association for
Humanistic Psychology & California State University Northridge, June 7, 2008

DECADE OF THE DREAM

The recent Decade of the Brain
I found was much too great a strain.
It burned mine out, and I am left
quite mindless and of hope bereft.

Now comes the Decade of the Gene,
a slogan that I find obscene.
I wish there were some persons still
who'd help me my frail dreams fulfill.

We need a Decade of the Dream
in which bright rays of hope would beam
down on our sordid human plight
and fill us with some healing light

MY SEARCH FOR MEANING

My musings are morose and murky,
querulous, quixotic, quirky,
seeking meekly for some meaning
so I can go on as Greening.
On most days I feebly fumble,
curse my fate and numbly grumble.
That is why my dog and I
usually see eye to eye,
and why he's given to remarking,
"What's the point of even barking?"

SISYPHUS REDUX

This rock, this mountain, this man,
this futile perseverance—
what use is such a myth?
Sisyphus gets nowhere,
gravity always wins.
Go ahead, if you wish—
imagine him happy
with or without anti-depressants.
You might as well imagine
the rock is ecstatic
bouncing down the slope, defiant.

So is this struggle any use to us?
We are in it, and outside it.
We view it, and have attitudes.
We are not rocks, not mountains,
not sure we are Sisyphus.
We read the story,
see him sweat,
dodge the rock,
respect the mountain,
climb up to stand on Sisyphus's shoulders
and peer beyond, beyond.

UNFAIR NEGLECT

I must say I get quite annoyed
when colleagues honor Sigmund Freud
instead of deifying *me*
as Father of Psychology.
Carl Rogers gets far too much praise,
which never ceases to amaze
me 'cause I really am quite sure
that I'm the one who best can cure.
Some oafs look up to Otto Rank--
For what do they have him to thank?
Mad febrile fools get in a frenzy
admiring old Sandor Ferenczi.
There's Maslow, Jung, and weird Fritz Perls,
around whom adulation swirls,
and other dolts, to my dismay,
pray piously to Rollo May,
while I, the wisest one of all.
am overshadowed by their gall
and left here spurned, alone, abject,
the victim of unfair neglect.
Thank God I have become inured
and know that someday when they're cured
they'll wake at last and know it's I
whom they should praise and deify.

PSYCHOPHARMACOPHOBIA

I wish that I could merely yawn and shrug
each time they peddle a new dandy drug,
as if the cure for basic human ills
can be supplied by pretty little pills.
Do these slick doctors honestly suppose
that thus they'll solve our existential woes?
Do they expect they'll get me to believe
that clever chemicals can fast relieve
the angst endemic to the human race
and put a cheery outlook in its place?
They try so hard to con us and convince
that I can only cower, quake and wince,
and if I blow my psychic thermostat
they'll offer me a magic pill for that.

POSITIVE PSYCHOLOGY ANTHEM

Let's revere these cheerful shrinks.
They are heroes whom we praise.
They're the ones who study happiness,
brighten up our darkest days.

They have theories and hard evidence
showing what can bring us cheer.
Put your faith in these psychologists
and you will have naught to fear.

Are you plagued by inhumanity,
misery you can't abide?
Triumph over life's dark tragedies,
celebrate the brighter side.

Never mind our insane president,
never mind the ghastly war.
Follow positive psychologists
to a brighter happy shore.

DIVERSITY?

Quite often out of sheer perversity
I take a stand against diversity.
I think we all should be the same
and thus it has become my aim
to make you be much more like me
so we can live quite tranquilly.
Diversity is too complex
and serves no purpose but to vex
wise elders who know how to be
content with phony harmony

VENTING

A colleague urged a group of us to eschew
"curmudgeonly venting not suitable for a
professional listserv."

I am a curmudgeon addicted to venting,
a tendency that I need help in preventing.
On days when I sink into feeling dysphoric
I find that my verses become sophomoric.
The bounds of good taste I repeatedly flout--
I count on my colleagues to straighten me out,

YOU CAN LEARN

Pity poet Thomas Greening--
he gave up the search for meaning
and instead does endless preening
and compulsive karma cleaning.
But he never will prevail,
so his life's a sorry tale.
He refuses to be good
and won't do the things he should.
Thus poor Tom careens downhill
while his antics count for nil.
You can learn from this dumb dope:
Give up sulking, do not mope,
try your best to stay awake,
and avoid poor Tom's mistake.

HARDY GENES

A friend suggested that I am blessed with hardy genes.

If my genes are really hardy
the benefits are very tardy.
I wait and wait for inspiration
but all I get is perspiration.
I'd like to trade my genes for yours
'cause I'm the sort who much prefers
to function as a normal dolt
instead of one who must revolt
against each regulation, law,
and all that's sticking in my craw.

I AM THE BEST

I am no good at optimism
because of my glum pessimism.
My outlook's always dark and dim,
my mood and my demeanor grim.
When others laugh I mope and moan
and much prefer to sulk alone.
I cringe at life and am aghast
to find my pleasures never last.
Alas, I've failed at narcissism
and, whimpering, flunked stoicism.
But there's one way I come in first:
I am the best at feeling worst.

WHY I AM REVERED

I must confess quite honestly
that I've transcended modesty.
The reason I am so revered
is that my verses have endeared
me to my yearning fellow man
from Brooklyn to the Yucatan.
To denigrate my poetry
is nothing short of blasphemy.
Who dares to do this, surely he
will suffer shame and infamy.
So woe to those who carp and snipe,
who relish other poets' tripe.
My stuff is best, as you can see--
please send me lots of flattery.

GOD'S POET

I am compelled to scoff and chortle
at those who wish to be immortal.
Quite clearly they have not discerned
that is a blessing to be earned.
These tiresome twits are such a bore--
it's I who will live evermore.
My wit and wisdom elevate me
and thus have come to designate me
to rise above this realm mundane
and as God's poet proudly reign.
If you object and claim I'm vain
you'll suffer more of His disdain,
for He's decreed that I'm a saint
and has no time for your complaint,
but if you want to be like me,
just emulate my modesty.

A SHOW OF MODESTY

It never ceases to amaze me
when sane adults admire and praise me.
I cannot see my own "pure light;"
I look within and just see blight.
Each time that I am complimented
I grow a little more demented.
The dissonance is just too great
and I know that I'm tempting fate.
If I believed the praise I get
I'd only mope, despair and fret
because I know that ere too long
I'll prove my complimenters wrong.
(If you fall for this show of modesty
I've fooled you with my sly dishonesty.)

HAVING AND GETTING

"Life is not a having and a getting
but a being and a becoming."
   - Matthew Arnold

If living is not about having and getting,
why am I so constantly whining and fretting,
and grasping and clutching at frivolous joys,
and counting my worth by the size of my toys?
If you knew me well you would easily see
"becoming" and "being" are miles beyond me.
It's all very simple for those more mature
to preach about values of which they are sure,
but what of we addicts who covet and crave?
Are all of us sadly too far gone to save?

IN DEFENSE OF DREARY

Some poets write verse that's enchanting,
while mine is mostly morbid ranting.
My friends indulge me, but complain
I stifle joy and dwell on pain.
I aggravate most everyone
but this is how I have my fun.
Tomorrow I will try to be more cheery
but now I cherish being dreary.

THE CRITICS ARE QUITE RIGHT

I think the critics are quite right--
my poetry is just a blight.
I recommend it all be junked
and I as tasteless fraud debunked.
The world is troubled quite enough
and does not want my noxious fluff.
Why dwell upon all that is dark?
Instead let's have ourselves a lark.
When life seems nasty, coarse and hard
we need a cheery Hallmark card.
From now on I will entertain
and hope it does not break my brain.

INCOMPETENT

Our grand profession needs vitality.
That is a stark and stern reality.
But please, I beg, don't look to me--
I am bemired in apathy.
It turns out I have faulty genes,
and you know what this bad news means:
I'll soon be drugged and dragged away
so I won't jinx psychology.
In modern times good shrinks must be
prepared to show their loyalty.
Forgive my gross incompetence,
timidity and diffidence.
Because I am inept and stodgy
I cannot help you torture Haji.

NUTS LIKE ME

If you put me in a cage
I will fly into a rage.
If you then dare let me out
I will sulk, mope, bleat and pout.
When you're faced with nuts like me
better just to let us free.
Harmlessly we'll rave and rant
at whatever is extant.

LESS THAN GREAT EXPECTATIONS

I longed to be a nerdy geek
but always have been far too meek.
I grumble, mourn and curse the fates
that did not make me like Bill Gates.
Instead I am conventional
and sadly one-dimensional.
I tried some drugs to get a high
but all I did was mope and sigh.
While others soar psychedelically
I cling to earth pathetically.
Now I'm resigned to yearn and pine,
and sip a glass of two buck wine.

HOW I WIN

My friend excels at being smart:
he's been a star right from the start.
He wins with skill, he wins with luck,
while I'm just a befuddled schmuck.
In life he's pulled out way ahead,
while I still fool around instead.
Since he was born he's always known
which car to drive, which house to own,
but there's one thing he doesn't know:
I am the best at letting go.
While he is driven to compete
I readily concede defeat.
I win the game of being cool,
and clearly am the wiser fool.

PUZZLED

My sense of humor is just rank
and overall I am a crank.
When lovers laugh it irritates me
and every little thing frustrates me.
I find my joy in others' grief
and scheme to steal my brother's fief.
I constantly must get my way
and never heed what critics say.
I don't want trouble, just to win.
So I'm a schmuck--is that a sin?
But still I'm puzzled by one fact:
Why am I constantly attacked?

DERVISH

A colleague described some of my poems as "scampish." I was offended, so wrote this.

I try hard to be boorish,
morose, bizarre and ghoulish.
I'm stubborn, mean and mulish,
and morbid verses cherish,
but get called merely "scampish,"
a small step up from "impish,"
and much too close to "foppish."
At least I am not foolish
or even vaguely vampish
when grievances I nourish.
Recalcitrant and selfish,
my stinging barbs are waspish.
My goal is to be churlish
and all my critics vanquish.
Forgive me if I'm snobbish,
but I'm a snarling dervish.

TRANSCENDING MY SELF

> To study the Way is to study the self.
> To study the self is to forget the self.
> To forget the self is to be enlightened.
>   - Dogen, founder of Zen in Japan

No longer do I flaunt my self.
I wisely left it on the shelf.
I do not need it any more—
It really had become a bore.

I walk about a freer man
delighted that at last I can
fly from attachments like a bird
and find my ego quite absurd.

I'm proud that I've achieved this goal
and hope you will admire my soul.
I praise myself as quite enlightened...
but still of nothingness am frightened.

MY BUDDHIST VOW

I've taken a most sacred vow:
I will surrender to the Tao.
That is the way I will succeed
in gratifying every need.
I'll grasp and clutch at happiness
and leave the world a dreadful mess.
My karma's cleansed, so I can do
whatever I may want to you.
If I have fears I might be wrong
I'll simply sing this cheerful song:
"The Buddha loves me, yes I know,
because my guru told me so."

PERMANENCE

About one thing I'm adamant:
Whatever is, is permanent.
Although some people think I'm strange,
I am against all social change.
Rash innovations jolt and jar--
let's keep things just the way they are.
If God wants progress, he can try.
He soon will see how we defy
his paltry efforts to upgrade
this paradise that we have made.
(I hope this verse will somehow please
my mentor, wise Parmenides.)

ASKING ANTS TO FLY

In my attempt to charm and please
I have become much like Swiss cheese.
I'm smooth and soft, but I have holes
where other people have their souls.

When called upon to be sincere
I just get overwhelmed by fear.
I mumble nonsense vapidly
and show my inner vacancy.

The prospect of becoming real
for me, alas, holds no appeal.
You might as well ask ants to fly,
though if you did I'd wonder why.

VACATION?

Much to my shock and consternation
a colleague took a real vacation,
so now I feel like quite a jerk
who thinks that life consists of work.
Nobody told me I might rest
and thus renew my long-lost zest.
We workaholics know no peace;
our great endeavors must not cease.
To save the world is no small task
and I can only humbly ask:
when we've perfected life on earth
could we take time for joy and mirth?

AS IF

I find it very sad to see
the state of our psychology.
Its views strike me as quite simplistic,
demeaning and reductionistic.
I'm sure that there is more to us
than anatomic incubus.
Psychologists who think like that
see me no different from a rat.
Of course, some days they may be right,
as when I feel compelled to fight
because they plan to steal my cheese,
or claim I have a brain disease.
I'm more than my neurology—
at least that's what I strive to be.
Let's visualize much higher goals:
Let's act as if we might have souls

OPENMINDEDNESS

I know that we are not supposed
to be recalcitrant or closed,
but it's my nature to resist
and in my stubborn way persist.
I'm always right, so feel required
to help you dolts who are bemired
in lower forms of consciousness
that cause you so much angst and stress.
The world will be a better place
when blessed by my inherent grace.
And as for you who disagree--
I will forgive your blasphemy.

AD HOMINEM

Ad hominem attacks are fun
when expertly and meanly done.
They are unfair and in bad taste
but never should be made in haste.
Your victim must be well impaled
and witnesses all be regaled
with accusations sly and cruel
to make him seem a dreadful fool.
It is an art to vilify
in ways you cannot justify.

WORK ETHIC

Let others loaf in lives bucolic--
I am a fervid workaholic.
I love to toil and labor long
and rant that idleness is wrong.
My friends regard me as a drone
while I prefer to sweat and groan.
But here is what does this load leaven:
I'm sure that I will go to heaven.
And if I don't, and land in hell
I'll tend those cauldrons very well.

REQUEST TO STUDENTS

Writing that's obtuse and vague
fulminates a dreadful plague.
Reading it is too much work—
teachers often go berserk.
Students have been crucified
when their prose is ossified.
Spare your readers brain meltdowns—
wisely choose your verbs and nouns.
Dense and convoluted prose
only makes us bellicose.
Just delete the fancy fluff—
simple syntax is enough.
Please indulge our urgent need—
write us prose that we can read.

FACULTY MEMO

The faculty of this famed institute
oft finds itself engaged in much dispute
about the proper way to run the place,
and how to do it with some sense of grace.

There are so many groups we try to please—
ourselves, the students, WASC and the trustees—
and thus, to teach psychology it seems
we must resort to rather drastic means.

The outcome of this strife is still unclear,
and this creates an anxious atmosphere,
so while we struggle with unwelcome stress
I thought perhaps it's time that I confess—

My mind is hardly fit for such discourse
and jumps about much like a skittish horse.
Just when my colleagues need me to be sane
I write these lines that really are inane.

But if my poem lightens up our mood
and makes us somewhat less inclined to brood,
then I will feel that I have done my part
to demonstrate the value of bad art.

FACULTY REVIEW

Let's keep this just twixt me and you–
I dread my faculty review.
Through yet another year I've fumbled,
too many weighty tasks I've bumbled.
My peers all tried to be supportive,
but my best efforts were abortive.
I waste my time in writing drivel,
when criticized I whine and snivel.
I quickly get on the defensive
and make remarks that are offensive.
Diversity eludes my brain
and tolerance I find a strain.
When talk with colleagues gets too deep
I cannot help but fall asleep.
I've tried to remedy these flaws
but constantly more self-doubt gnaws
away at what was once my pride
and I just want to flee and hide.
To keep my tattered record clean
I guess I'll have to bribe the Dean.

PROFESSORIAT

I really am delighted that
I'm in a professoriat.
For years I wandered all alone
in hopes that I would find my clone.
Now I have found some folks like me
and we preach wisdom righteously.
We know we're right and others wrong,
and which folks in our clique belong.
We're truly smarter than the mob;
dispensing truth is our hard job.
We do it well and you will see
we soon will save humanity.

MARTYR'S COMPLAINT

I have a serious complaint:
I have not yet been made a saint.
I suffer, writhe, kvetch, shriek and moan,
but sadly do this all alone.
Why do I never cease to whine?
No cult has made for me a shrine.
I'm lonely in my bleak despair
and no one really seems to care,
but I'll say this about my plight:
When I complain I do it right.
I have succeeded in my quest:
At suffering I am the best.

WILLIAM JAMES?

I have a friend who vainly claims
that he himself is William James.
Now frankly, if the truth be told,
that fact would make him very old.
Two things about him that are weird:
He really does have James' big beard,
and views our cruel world through the lens
of multiple entheogens.
He lives in Cambridge, as did James,
and from his high horse bluntly blames
the sad state of psychology
on lesser beings such as me
because I, beardless, prefer malls
to academia's hallowed halls.

THE NEGLECTED WORKS OF ARTHUR BOHART

Although I am grateful to Art Bohart for his Preface to this book, my
dwindling intellectual integrity compelled to write this poem.

And why, you ask, are they neglected?
For reasons that must be respected.
He writes too much that is arcane
and often seems just plain inane.
He claims that therapy can heal
and makes great efforts to reveal
how that strange process comes about
but leaves me puzzled and in doubt
because it never worked for me,
as those who know me all can see.
Perhaps some day this guy Bohart,
who thinks he is so very smart,
will cook up some new therapy
to cure me of my lunacy.
"What a relief," the world will cry,
but then they'll see, as time goes by,
that I am only slightly nuts,
but Bohart still is a big putz.

FOR RONNIE LAING

Who's mad and who's sane,
and who decides?
If you have to ask,
don't ask out loud,
or you could end up
on the wrong side of the keys,
knife, chemicals, or electricity.
What was a nice Scottish doctor
doing in a world like this?
Rattling paradigms, that's what,
and drinking more than he should.
His time is up,
and the psychiatric pub
is quieter now.
Once he asked,
"Where in the world
are lunatics allowed to bathe
naked in the moonlight?"
At last he has found the place,
but he's probably splashing
more than God allows.

FOR JIM BUGENTAL

Authentic persons everywhere,
Be empathetic, show you care,
Transcend your existential guilt,
Don't let your will to meaning wilt,
Turn off TV, forsake the mall,
Come honor our Jim Bugental.
Though he has been here eight decades
His brilliance never dims or fades.
It's he who guides us straight and true,
Who sees the soul in each of you.
But who's behind those books of his?
It's not some wizard, no—it's Liz!
So let us cheer and celebrate
These lovebirds whom we think are great.

HOORAY, HOORAY FOR ROLLO MAY

Back in '58 I bought
a book on existential thought.
Little did I know, of course,
that this fine book would be the source
of this occasion here today
at which we honor Rollo May.

Those of us who raptly follow
words and thoughts from our friend Rollo
know he has a vast potential
to cure our crises existential.
If your temperament's dystonic
he'll turn you on to the daimonic.
If you've got a void to fill
he'll strengthen both your love and will.
Depressed about the slim results
you've gotten when you've joined those cults?
Here's the man who'll guarantee
there's meaning in anxiety.
If your mood is turning dour
it's innocence you need, and power.
He's got a book about those too--
he's really written quite a few.
A shrink who reads and quotes Lord Byron,
who knows how to escape a siren,
the Lapps all loudly sing his praise
for ridding Lapland of malaise.
In Russian, where he's read a lot,
they publish him in Samizdat.

His home is perched above the bay,
half way to heaven, some would day.
And yet, of course, he's not a saint,
flawed as he is by just one taint--
Clandestinely, when no one looks,

he plagiarizes from my books.
But if you find that life's a bummer,
let this man be your distant drummer.

Here's to this scholar distingue,
here's to our mentor, Rollo May.

Read at the Saybrook National Meeting, January 1985.

A TRIBUTE TO ROLLO MAY

As an undergraduate I couldn't decide between majoring in psychology and literature, so I created a program for myself with a muddled combination of the two. One year I learned about existentialism in a course on French novels, and about psychology in a course on rats. In graduate school I found it prudent to remain a closet existentialist. I wish I'd known then that Rollo May and others were in the process of creating a psychology about people that integrated existentialism.

The year I got my PhD, 1958, Rollo published *Existence: A New Dimension in Psychiatry and Psychology*. Jim Bugental and Al Lasko, whom I had joined in their group practice, thought this was an important book. At last it was safe for me to "come out." No longer did I have to slink around bars searching for furtive existentialist conversations with strangers. I could be a psychologist and an existentialist. I could openly display my Camus and Sartre books in my office. I even published existentially oriented articles under my real name. It was Rollo May who opened me up to the ontological dimension of psychotherapy and readied me for the subsequent influence of Herbert R. Lochenkopf, and the austere challenges of Exitism. To express my gratitude, I offer this tribute:

A remarkable fellow named Rollo,
When told that existence is hollow,
Said, "There's nothing amiss,
We can fill the abyss,"
And gave us directions to follow.

ROLLO COMES OF AGE

Rollo May celebrated his 85th birthday in April 1994. Maria Watts of Saybrook Institute arranged a small party for him at a waterfront restaurant in Sausalito with a beautiful view of the San Francisco Bay. I told Rollo I wished I could arrange an historic meeting between him and Solzhenitsyn before he returned to Russia, twenty years after being deported. What might these two visionary men have to say to each other? I spoke of the relevance of Rollo's latest book, *The Cry for Myth*, to Russia today, and of his discussion of *Oedipus at Colonus* in which the blind old man has achieved much sought-after wisdom and the capacity to love. As an example of transcendent existential commitment to creativity in the face of chaos and the daimonic, I quoted Solzhenitsyn's statement as he contemplated his return: "I know that I will be torn apart by people's tragedies and the events of the time." Rollo said that the book that needs to be written is an exploration of the relevance of the great Russian literature, especially Tolstoy and Dostoyevsky, to the struggle of Russia and indeed the world today,

By then the sun has set and it was time for dessert and frivolity.

A few years back we joined to say,
"Hooray, Hooray for Rollo May,"
but there's a fact we can't deny:
Our tempus fugit, and goes by.
Once more his birthday's come around,
so let's all try to be profound.
Our Rollo's really come of age--
This kid's become a grown up sage!
In spite of Angst he's learned to thrive
and reached the age of 85.
He wrote some books and tried to paint,
but sad to say he is no saint.
I'll skip the details of his sins--
It isn't how one's life begins
in dark daimonic storms and strife,
but how one lives the rest of life.
When he was young he broke some rule
and got himself thrown out of school.

Soon he reformed, earned a degree,
and thought he'd try the ministry.
They made him pastor of a church,
but he had just begun his search,
and though he had a family,
decided he'd prefer TB.
This holiday helped him to see
the meaning of anxiety,
and thus he turned a dread disease
into a source of royalties.
Eventually he wandered west,
and so it is that we are blessed.
His scribbling culminated with
a treatise on the cry for myth.
Let's celebrate Paul Tillich's heir
who wrote his way out of despair.
Salute Dasein's distinguished don--
All hail the Sage of Tiburon!

Read at Rollo's 85th birthday party, April 1994.

ROLLUSHKA

Georgia May told me that a Russian friend had given Rollo the
nickname "Rollushka." It seemed to me that there should be a poem on
that theme, but what could possibly rhyme with "Rollushka?" All I could
think of was "Babushka," and I could not imagine a poem linking Rollo
with such a traditional Russian personage. The unconscious went to
work, however, and in the middle of the night I produced the final poem
in this literary debacle.

> There she sits so old and sad--
> Have pity on the poor babushka.
> Life is grim in Petrograd,
> but she is cheered by our Rollushka
>
> He redeems her Slavic gloom,
> and gives her existential meaning,
> brightens up her dreary room,
> and offers her a karmic cleaning.
>
> Russian nights are cold and grim,
> and Russian hearts are plagued with malice,
> so she turns her soul toward him--
> Rollushka always gives her solace.
>
> When she pines and cries for myth
> dear Rollo writes a book about it.
> Thus his words provide her with
> a faith so strong she'll never doubt it.
>
> Stalin's gone, Khrushchev is dead,
> and Lenin failed our poor babushka.
> Whom should she revere instead?
> Let's crown as Czar the great Rollushka!

ROLLO MAY
1909-1994

No need for us to feel downhearted
because our Rollo has departed.
The searching artist now can rest
in the fulfillment of his quest.
As he ascends, we can rejoice
that he is soothed by Beauty's voice.
Transcending our poor earthly grief,
let us imagine God's relief
to have in heaven such a man
to help him thwart the Devil's plan.
Dear Rollo now is God's resource
for channeling daimonic force
to aid us sinners left behind,
as Huxley urged, to be more kind.

Read at Rollo's memorial service at Grace Cathedral, October 29,
1994.

New Poems

I'VE TRIED TO STOP

My doggerel keeps getting worse,
so readers are of course averse
to my sick need to poetize,
and now are loath to sympathize.
I've tried to stop, give up vain scribbling,
abandon my incessant quibbling
about which word I ought to use,
and thus my friends' goodwill abuse.
But I don't know what else to do,
besides inflict these poems on you.
Perhaps shrinks can suggest some drug,
or find a way to pull the plug.

FRAGMENTS

A poem can easily fall off the shelf
and break, and there is no glue
that will fix it.
Believe me—I have hundreds of fragments.
Why don't I just throw them away?
They cannot be melted down and recast.
Sometimes I put them at the bottom of flower pots
so roots won't rot from too much water.
Maybe when I get enough I will use them
to make a gravel path from my house
to the edge of earth.

BLIZZARD

Waiting for the snowplow,
I just sit in the kitchen
with my hat on and my parka zipped up.
It is so quiet I can hear my dog breathe.
I've done my part: got up, got ready.
No one can blame me for being late.
I could wash the dishes, make phone calls,
but I just sit, warm,
welcoming the snow.
The six foot drift in my driveway
is my comforter.
By noon I realize
that the plow will never come,
that it is August,
and that I am finally
at peace.

DOG STORY

We don't need weird foreigners
or sadistic strangers
to demonstrate how to be cruel.
Henry's own older brothers did it–
poured gasoline on his dog,
set it afire,
and roared with laughter
as it ran, a four-legged torch,
around the backyard
until it collapsed
and Henry went mad.

SISYPHUS'S SOLUTION

It often has occurred to me:
life's tougher than it ought to be.
Poor Sisyphus, assigned a chore
which was quite weighty and a bore,
found a solution, clever, drastic:
He made a rock of lightweight plastic.
If you've a boring job you hate,
if you are burdened by some weight,
think long and hard—perhaps you too
can think of something sly to do.

DOUBT

So often have I let my standards fall–
how can I claim some self-respect at all?
While others strove for common decency
I grasped and grabbed with greed and gluttony.
Thus what grim future is in store for me?
Can I still salvage shreds of decency?
I'll pray to God–just tell me which one's best
and will consent to aid me in my quest.
I'm hopeful that there's one who will help out,
but sometimes I am overcome by doubt.

SPRINGTIME WITH CHAUCER

Where's Chaucer to sing praise of April's showers,
to celebrate her fresh cascades of flowers?
This tardy springtime needs a lyric writer,
a bard who makes our dreary world glow brighter.
If left to me you'd get no verse romantic;
instead I'd crank out lines obtuse, pedantic,
botanic lore and scientific facts,
dull prose that sadly inspiration lacks.
Though good old Geoffrey long ago departed,
we pilgrims need not languish here downhearted.
If you want verse that tickles and regales
just read aloud his Canterbury Tales.

WAIT AND SEE

Am I a saint, or vile, obscene?
The truth is somewhere in between.
I don't behave the way I should,
my best is often none too good.
When asked to choose a higher way
I find I want to disobey.
What will become of wayward me?
All we can do is wait and see.
In any case, I'd like to state
I don't deserve your rabid hate.

BRING SOME SENSE

Grasping, clutching, craving meaning,
in its absence howling, keening,
here we pace like some crazed beast
mourning for a world that ceased.
Bring fresh sense into our life,
peace instead of mindless strife.
Give us some new raison d'etre
quench the raging storms of hate, or
show a path for our redemption,
from this hell— a circumvention.

BARKING

Other people have knowledge,
informed opinions.
I envy them.
They know whom to vote for,
how to choose good wine,
what to do about the Middle East.
I went to college, and I subscribe
to *The Nation, The New Yorker, The New York Times*,
but can never figure out what to believe,
whom to trust, hate.
My dog is similarly limited,
but deals with it by barking.
When I develop some confidence
I will bark more.

STAY ALERT

There's much about this country you abhor,
and so you plan to move to Ecuador.
Before you go, however, you should know
adopting to a new land may be slow.
Although it has a very different name
some of its drawbacks are perhaps the same.
Wherever human beings congregate
they manage to stir up much fear and hate,
so stay alert and you won't be surprised–
May all your hopes and dreams be realized.

A REQUEST

Forgive me–I must ask you please–
pen poems I can read with ease,
not jerky ones that make me stumble.
I know my own are crude and humble
but I had hoped to count on you
for lilting verses that renew
my faith that language can shine bright
when bards bring grace to what they write.
Erase the line twixt prose and song–
it's melody for which we long.

STOP TIME

Blindsided, I did not see it coming.
I suddenly got old.
Aging hit me hard.
Reeling, stumbling, shuffling,
tottering, lurching toward oblivion–
not a fun journey.
I've lost my return ticket,
forgotten which train to take,
hope I find one that stops in Venice
so I can stroll at sunset by canals,
have tea with Aschenbach and Tadzio,
and stop time.

DSM WHATEVER

My florid, wild pathology
was too much for DSM-3
My rampant symptoms were way more
than listed in DSM-4.
According to DSM-5
I really should not be alive.
I'm glad that docs create these books
to diagnose us weirdo kooks.
It's part of our creative nature
to make such crazy nomenclature.

BLAME OUR BRAINS

If I could find love, peace and stillness
might it subdue my "mental illness,"
or should I count on corporations
to dowse my brain with their solutions?
The cost of sanity is high
and I have found the reason why:
Executives must live in style
and thus they cleverly beguile
we crazies who consume their pills
to blame our brains for all our ills.

CONFESSION OF A TROLL

The day I stopped my medication
my friends recoiled in consternation.
They have no faith at all in me
and treat me like an enemy.
It's true that I sometimes explode
or act like a repulsive toad,
a crazy and malignant troll,
who lacks the semblance of a soul.
I seldom act the way I should,
but way down deep I'm kind and good.

KEEP YOUR PILLS

I'm desperately dedicated
to being under-medicated.
Although this puts a dreadful strain
on my poor psychopathic brain,
I fear those quirky chemicals
will bring about no miracles
and will instead rot what is there,
thus causing me still more despair.
So keep your pretty little pills–
I'll keep my existential ills.

SIDE EFFECTS

My brain is full of gross defects
and thus I'm prone to side effects.
It's my own fault that I am nuts—
that's true, with no ifs, ands, or buts.
Nice doctors did their very best
but my weird demons never rest.
God bless all wise psychiatry—
it works for everyone but me.
I still have hopes they'll find a pill
to cure whatever makes me ill,
but if they don't, I'll know they tried,
and certainly have never lied.
So why claim that I gullibly
believe in their chicanery?

WHAT IS WRONG?

I must dispute my diagnosis
'cause what I have is not psychosis.
I simply am a little odd,
a rescuer sent here by God
to straighten out you errant fools
and ward off psychiatric ghouls
who'd like to make you dolts suspect
that in my brain there's some defect.
So what is wrong? Here is a clue:
The madness is in all of you.

DESPERATE SCRIBBLING

To ward off looming stark insanity
I've turned to writing verbose poetry.
I hope to keep from going mad
by scribbling couplets on a pad.
I fear this all may be in vain
and I will still become insane,
but on I write in desperation,
besieged by maddening frustration.
Can you assure me that some day
I'll save myself this quirky way?

NEGLIGENCE

All the books I never wrote,
all the times I failed to vote,
pretty girls I never kissed,
great performances I missed
haunt me now in my old age,
fuel my self-directed rage.
Forgive me my gross negligence–
I will show more deference
to life's rich contingencies,
thus the gods I may still please.

FLY LIKE AN ANGEL

I'm falling to earth in warm spring air,
through cumulus clouds, defeat and despair.
Earth looms below, welcoming me,
and my delusion that I am free.
But this will end, as all flights do–
pray it's an ending I'll share with you.
Gravity stalks us, humbles and thwarts,
treats us like rabble while breaking our hearts.
Fly like an angel as long as you can–
too soon you'll discover you're only a man.

OUR LEGACY

Let's weigh the facts a little more
before we launch another war.
Are we so sure we're in the right
and blessed by God to launch this fight,
and is cruel war the only way
triumphantly to seize the day?
Let he who lives devoid of sin
proclaim who righteously should win.
Survey all human history–
Is blindness our main legacy?

I'M PROUD

Please do not call me xenophobic–
I'm proud to say I'm patriotic
and confident I know who's good
and how our politicians should
conduct themselves to save our nation
from floods of rampant immigration.
Just build a wall with spikes on top–
that's how we'll this invasion stop.
And think how great our land will be
when everyone is just like me!

HOW TO BECOME REAL?

I'm much upset and bothered with
the fear that I am just a myth.
I thought God offered me a deal
that somehow I would be quite real.
He let me down, and all I get
is fantasy, and thus I fret,
and fumble, frown, and fulminate,
which hardly helps my angst abate.
Perhaps with Satan I can deal–
What must I do to become real?

SITTING WITH DOG

As I near the end of my life
I am proud to say that I've become able
to sit still for hours
with my dachshund asleep on my lap,
his nose tucked under my arm.
He taught me to do this.
Although at first I was a restless student,
his patience prevailed
and I am sitting here now
more at peace than I have ever been,
sheltered from the storms of regret,
hope and despair, seeking and striving.
But my attempt to write this poem
has disturbed him,
so I will stop and go back to just sitting,
breathing in rhythm with my nuzzling comrade
on our last journey.

POET'S PLEA

"And it was this month that my book of poems was coming out!
What attention will it get with this going on? What has
happened to England? Why don't they stop the war?"
   Amy Lowell

We poets have a stressful task
so hope it's not too much to ask
that governments demur before
they hastily begin a war.
Our readers, too, need peace and time
to scan our musings set to rhyme.
Please postpone wars when're you can,
perhaps impose a stringent ban
on bombing people whom we need
our precious poetry to read.

About the Author

Tom Greening studied psychology at Yale, the University of Vienna, and the University of Michigan, but didn't learn much. Nevertheless, he has practiced psychotherapy in the same office for 50 years. He was Editor of the Journal of Humanistic Psychology for 35 years, and that may have affected his sanity. He is a clinical professor at UCLA and Professor Emeritus at Saybrook Graduate School. In college he read too much Chaucer, Pope, and Dryden, thereby becoming addicted to rhyming couplets. One of his narcissistic goals is to upstage Ogden Nash, while still paying tribute to him:

Cultures may crumble, titans may crash.
We'll always have Paris, and dear Ogden Nash.

Since the original publication of *Words Against the Void*, Dr. Greening has been quite prolific, publishing *Poems For and About Elders* (Revised & Expanded Edition), *Our Last Walk: Using Poetry for Remembering and Grieving Our Pets* (with Louis Hoffman & Michael Moats), *Nasreddin the Psychologist*, and *Animals I Have Known*.

Other Books by Tom Greening

Poems For and About Elders (Revised & Expanded Edition)

Our Last Walk: Using Poetry for Grieving and Remembering Our Pets (with Louis Hoffman & Michael Moats)

Animals I Have Known

Nasreddin the Psychologist

Other Books by University Professors Press

Stay Awhile: Poetic Narratives on Multiculturalism and Diversity
By Louis Hoffman and Nathaniel Granger, Jr.

Capturing Shadows: Poetic Encounters Along the Path of Grief and Loss
By Louis Hoffman & Michael Moats

Journey of the Wounded Soul: Poetic Companions for Spiritual Struggles
By Louis Hoffman & Steve Fehl

An Artist's Thought Book: Intriguing Thoughts About the Artistic Process (2nd Edition)
By Richard Bargdill

Stanley Krippner: A Life of Dreams, Myths, & Visions
By Jeannine A. Davies and Daniel B. Pitchford

The Polarized Mind: Why It's Killing Us and What We Can Do About It
By Kirk J. Schneider

Humanistic Contributions for Psychology 101: Growth, Choice, and Responsibility
By Richard Bargdill & Rodger Broomé

Bare: Psychotherapy Stripped
By Jacqueline Simon Gunn & Carlo DeCarlo

www.ingramcontent.com/pod-product-compliance
Lightning Source LLC
Chambersburg PA
CBHW021403090426
42742CB00009B/989